GROWING UP IN THE
THIRTIES

Rebecca Hunter

HODDER
Wayland

an imprint of Hodder Children's Books

Produced for Hodder Wayland by
Discovery Books Ltd
Unit 3, 37 Watling Street, Leintwardine, Shropshire SY7 0LW, England

First published in 2001 by Hodder Wayland, an imprint of Hodder Children's Books

British Library Cataloguing in Publication Data

Hunter, Rebecca,
    Growing up in the thirties
    1. Children - Great Britain - Social life and customs -
    Juvenile literature 2. Great Britain - Social conditions -
    20th century - Juvenile literature 3. Great Britain - Social
    life and customs - 1918-1945 - Juvenile literature
    I. Title
    941 ' . 083 ' 0922

    ISBN 0 7502 3433 4

Printed and bound in Grafiasa, Porto, Portugal.

Designer: Ian Winton
Editor: Rebecca Hunter

Hodder Children's Books would like to thank the following for the loan of their material:
Birds Eye Wall's Ltd: page 13 (bottom); **Glasgow Museum of Transport**: page 27, 29;
Hulton Getty: page 6 (top), 8, 10 (top) Humphrey Spender, 14 (top) Richards, 15 (top), 16
(bottom), 18 (top), 19 (bottom) Fred Morley, 21 (top), Reg Speller, 30 (top), cover (left);
Lambeth Archives Department: page 6 (bottom); **Museum of Welsh Life**: page 12;
The Advertising Archives: page 11 (top); **The Leicester Mercury**: page 26 (bottom), 28 (top);
The Robert Opie Collection: page 7 (bottom), 9 (top), 20 (right),
21 (bottom), 24 (bottom), cover (centre).

Hodder Children's Books
A division of Hodder Headline Limited
338 Euston Road
London NW1 3BH

CONTENTS

THE 1930s

The 1930s were a time of worldwide recession called the Depression. Many men were unemployed and families had very little money to spend. As if the Depression weren't enough, by the end of the 1930s everyone's lives changed as the Second World War began. In this book, five people who grew up in thirties Britain tell what their lives were like during these difficult times.

NORMAN KIES

Norman was born in 1929 in Central London. His father was a baker and he lived with his parents and sister in South London.

▶ Norman in 1934 aged 5.

BOB DOWNEY

Bob was born in 1924, the youngest of three brothers. His father was a shopkeeper and they lived in Sudbury, a small town in Suffolk.

▶ Bob in 1931 aged 7.

JOYCE BIRD

Joyce grew up in West Ealing, London. She was born in 1923. Her grandfather, father and uncle ran an ironmonger's business with several shops in London.

▶ Joyce in 1935 aged 12.

ARTHUR HOUSTON

Arthur was born in 1928 in Scotland. His father was a solicitor and his mother a doctor. He was the eldest of four children and the family lived in the west end of Glasgow.

▶ Arthur in 1937 aged 9.

SHEILA WALKER

Sheila grew up in a small village in South Wales called Llwynhendy. She was born in 1924 and had two older brothers.

▶ Sheila in 1936 aged 12.

THE DEPRESSION

The Depression was the name given to the early years of the 1930s. It was a time when the country was going through a period of great hardship. Nobody had money to buy goods and many industries suffered. Large numbers of men lost their jobs. Those people who did have jobs worked for very low wages and living conditions were very different from what we are used to today.

Two unemployed men gaze at the factory where they used to work.

HOUSES

Few homes in the thirties had modern conveniences like electric washing machines or refrigerators. Cities were still full of old slum houses with many families living in one-room flats with no indoor bathroom. Most people rented their homes; very few were owned.

THEN & NOW

- The average weekly wage for men in 1938 was £2 13s 3d (£2.66). In 1998 it was £383.

- An average house in the 1930s cost about £800. In 1999 it was £92,500.

Bob

We lived in an old house behind my dad's shop. The house had no bathroom and it only had electricity downstairs. We used candles and oil lights upstairs. There was no central heating or hot water and it was very cold in winter. This picture shows the town of Sudbury where we lived.

Between 1934 and 1939 local councils pulled down over 250,000 slum houses. In their place they built new council housing estates or blocks of flats.

New homes were built in the wealthier suburbs. A typical 1930s house had bay-fronted windows and a garden. For the first time ordinary families were able to borrow money with a mortgage to buy a home of their own.

GAS AND ELECTRICITY

Up until the 1930s, most houses had gas lights, because there was no electricity. The streets were also lit by gas lamps which had to be lit every evening by a lamp lighter.

Arthur

Just before dark the lamp lighter would walk up and down every street lighting the lamps. He carried a long pole with a gas flame at the top. The pole had a lever so that he could open the gas tap. Early in the morning the lamp lighter had to do the rounds again, putting out the lights.

One of the things that changed people's lives most in the 1930s was electricity. A national grid system of cables and pylons was built across the country. Many new power stations were opened. The power stations were powered by coal. By 1937, nine million people had electricity in their homes.

Electricity pylons and cables spread across the countryside.

Electricity made a big difference everywhere. Electric lights replaced gas ones in the streets and traffic lights were introduced. Electric trains started to replace steam, and more electric trams were used. Factories used electricity to work machines and electrical goods like vacuum cleaners and washing machines became available to some people.

ELECTRICITY – BEST ALL WAYS

THE 'COUNTY' FIVE

CASH PRICE 11/6

CASH PRICE 19/6

CASH PRICE 33/-

CASH PRICE 13/9

CASH PRICE 19/6

The extra comforts which electrical services provide

The COUNTY OF LONDON ELECTRIC SUPPLY Co Ltd

Obtainable at Local Showrooms

You must move with the times Convenient payments arranged

An advert for some of the earliest electric appliances.

Joyce

As well as gardening tools and other household items, my dad's shop also made and sold the new, electric 'wireless set'. During the school holidays my brother and I helped in the shop. We were allowed to sell firewood and batteries, and weigh out nails and screws. Here is a picture of the shop with the tricycle that was used for deliveries. This shop eventually had to be knocked down for the building of the M4 motorway.

HOME LIFE

HOUSEWORK

Most women did not work once they were married. They stayed at home and looked after their homes and families. Few households had electric machines in the thirties, so keeping the house clean took much longer than today and women often did housework all day.

Washing machines were rare and so clothes and sheets were washed by hand. They would then be put through a mangle to squeeze out the water. There were no tumble dryers so all laundry was hung outside to dry, or, if it was raining, around the stove.

Bob

My mum did not go out to work, but I remember she was always busy. On Mondays she did the washing in a large copper in the corner of the kitchen. Ironing was done with two steel irons that were heated up on the gas ring. Mum was always cooking - making jams or bottling fruit. She also made delicious bread, cakes and pies - her apple and blackberry tart was my favourite.

DOMESTIC STAFF

In the 1930s many people were employed as domestic staff in town houses. People in domestic service were often quite well looked after but had to work very hard. They usually had one half day off a week, and perhaps a weekend once a month.

Arthur

My family had three members of staff: a cook, a maid and a nanny. Cook was Irish, fat and very jolly. I never saw Cook use a recipe book, she just seemed to produce delicious meals out of her head. My brother and sisters and I used to sneak into the kitchen to see what she was baking. We were often chased out with a broom!

THEN & NOW

• In the thirties it would have taken a housewife most of the day to do the washing. Now it takes only a few minutes to fill and empty the machine.

SHOPPING

In the early 1930s few people had refrigerators so they had to shop every day. There were no supermarkets and most shopping was done at small local shops or at the market. Food was bought fresh or in cans or jars. There was no frozen food. Perishable goods such as milk, butter and meat had to be kept in ice bought from the fishmonger, or stored in a cool larder. Dried goods like flour, rice and biscuits did not come in packets, but were weighed out and wrapped in paper.

Fruit and vegetables were always bought fresh, often from a market stall.

Old Money

Before decimalization, British currency was made up of pounds, shillings and pence. There were twelve pence (12d) in a shilling (5p today), and twenty shillings (20/-) in a pound. There were many more types of coins and bank notes. There was a one pound note and a ten shilling (50p) note.

Many shops delivered to the door.

Joyce

We lived **20** minutes away from the shops. Luckily the tradesmen called at home often. The baker came daily, the milkman several times a day and the greengrocer twice a week. Most produce was only available during the relevant season: fresh vegetables in the summer and fruits in the autumn. At other times of the year fruit and vegetables were bottled, dried or salted. In summer we waited for the ice cream tricycle to come by. The salesman rang a bell and called out 'Stop me and buy one.' My favourite ice cream was an orange snofrute. It cost one penny (less than ¹/2p) and came in a waxed cardboard wrapper.

THEN & NOW

• In the 1930s a loaf of bread cost about 4d (less than 2p). Today a loaf costs between 40p and 80p.

• In 1931 a typical housewife spent £2 12s 6d (£2.63) a week, on housekeeping. Now it would cost her over £100.

SCHOOL

In the 1930s, children had to go to school from age 5 to 14. Most children went to mixed council schools, which had 3 classes: infants, juniors and seniors.

Bob

The teachers at my school were very strict. If you made a mistake in spelling or English, you had to write 100 lines of the thing you got wrong. Sometimes we were smacked on the head or whacked with a ruler across the hand. If you were really naughty, you were sent to the head master to be caned.

Classrooms were often dull. There were few bright posters on the walls, and the furniture was wooden or metal and very practical. Each child had his or her own desk facing the front of the class, and nobody was allowed to talk during lessons. Most time was spent on reading, writing and arithmetic.

This picture shows some of the boys from Bob's class in the playground. The girls played in a different playground!

EXERCISE

Schools did not have the playing fields or gyms that they do today. Games such as football would be played in the playground or at the local recreation ground.

Sheila

Saint David is the patron saint of Wales, and every year on 1 March, our school celebrated Saint David's Day by putting on a performance. Each class had to perform a concert piece. Here is my class' group photo. I am sitting in the centre.

LEAVING SCHOOL

Some children went on to grammar schools or the high school but most had to leave school at 14 to find work.

HEALTH

Healthcare in the thirties was not as good as it is today. There was no National Health Service and most visits to the doctor cost money, so poor people rarely saw a doctor.

Arthur

My mother insisted that fresh air was good for you. My brother and sister and I were dressed up and taken for a walk every day - whatever the weather!

Children did not have injections to protect them against childhood diseases and often got ill. When one child in a school class came down with an illness, the other children had to be put in 'quarantine' and were sent home for two weeks.

A nurse comforts a child in hospital.

TUBERCULOSIS

One very serious disease was tuberculosis or TB. This was very infectious and children who had it had to be kept apart from the other children.

Pasteurized milk was introduced which was supposed to prevent the spread of TB.

Norman

There was one classroom at our school with open sides and canvas screens where the tuberculosis children were taught. We never got to know them as they never mixed with the rest of the school.

This picture, showing Norman's sister, was a winning entry in a competition run by the dairy industry. They wanted to promote how healthy pasteurized milk was, and sponsored many 'Bonny Baby' competitions.

THEN & NOW

• In the 30s, the number of cases of measles reported was over 400,000 a year. Now there are less than 7,500 a year.

Having Fun

Toys and Games

Although children had far fewer toys in the 1930s they had fun making up their own games. Because there was so little traffic it was safe for children to play in the streets. Hopscotch squares were chalked onto the paving stones using different coloured chalks. Running with a hoop and stick was also a popular game. You had to see how long you could keep your hoop moving.

Joyce

My brother Dennis and I did not have many toys, so those we had were carefully treasured. These pictures show my dolls' house and my brother's clockwork tin-plate train set.

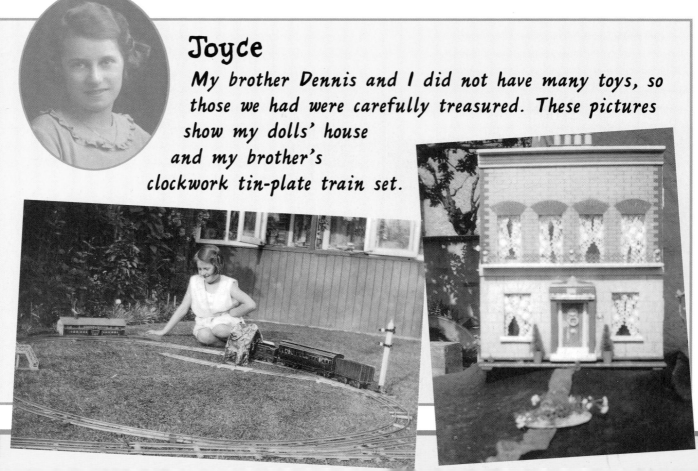

Norman

My sister and I enjoyed blowing bubbles. We dipped our bubble pipes into a tin of soapy water.

POCKET MONEY

Children spent their pocket money at the local corner shop. Sweets such as jelly babies, aniseed balls or dolly mixtures were sold from big glass jars. They were weighed out into 2oz, 4oz and 8oz (50g, 110g and 225g) measures. Other sweets like gob stoppers or sherbet dabs were sold from a penny tray or a half-penny tray.

COMICS

Comics such as the *Dandy* or the *Eagle* cost one penny. Children would often try and read a whole comic in the shop while the shopkeeper was busy with other customers, and then buy another one to take home!

THE WIRELESS

In 1936 the BBC started the first British television service, but since very few people had a television, not many were able to watch it. People got their entertainment by listening to the wireless. Wireless sets were quite expensive, costing about £20, but most homes had one.

Bob

We had a dome-shaped wireless made of Bakelite, an early sort of plastic. It had two batteries, one was a dry battery and the other was an accumulator wet battery that needed recharging. It was my job to take the accumulator to a wireless shop for charging.

▶ Gracie Fields was a very well known singer in the 1930s.

CINEMA

The cinema was a popular form of entertainment in the thirties. On Saturday mornings the cinemas opened for children only. Children called this 'Saturday morning pictures'. The programmes only cost one penny (less than $^1/2$p) and children queued to watch films like *Tarzan* or a weekly serial such as *Flash Gordon*.

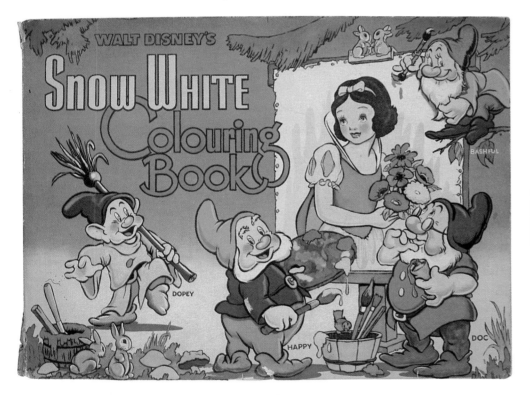

THEN & NOW

- A cinema show in the thirties consisted of two movies and a newsreel. Now they usually show just one film.

- Cinemas then had only one screen, there were no multiplexes.

The first full length Disney film to be made was *Snow White and the Seven Dwarfs*.

In 1938 Walt Disney started making colour cartoons. Mickey Mouse was the star of the first cartoon to have words and music and has been a children's favourite ever since.

HOLIDAYS

Holidays were rare for most people in the thirties. People couldn't afford them, transport was difficult and nobody had paid leave from work until 1938.

Norman

In 1935, 'school journeys' were introduced by the government. They were holiday breaks for children who would not otherwise ever have a holiday. Often children would be sent to stay on a farm in the country.

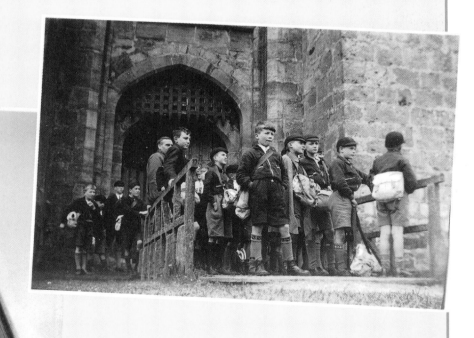

Our school went on one such holiday in 1937. We went to East Sussex. These pictures show us visiting Bodiam Castle and having fun at the Hastings swimming baths.

THE BEACH

People who could take holidays or day trips usually went to the beach. Brighton, Blackpool, Southend and Skegness were popular resorts.

Joyce

*Our luggage was always sent on in advance for our holidays. The trunks would be marked with a large label saying **PLA** which stood for Passenger Luggage in Advance. They were collected by the horse-drawn van of the Southern Railway Company and taken to the station to be put on a train to Dorset where we spent our holidays.*

People dressed very formally on the beach. Unless they were swimming, men kept their suits and caps on! Most people just paddled - not many had ever learned to swim. Children enjoyed their days on the beach playing cricket, making sand castles and watching Punch and Judy shows.

Sheila

We had relatives who lived in a pretty seaside village in Pembrokeshire. We sometimes took short holidays there. This picture shows me and my family on the beach.

Norman

The first holiday I went on was to the Isle of Wight. We travelled there by train. When we got to the

island, we stayed in a boarding house. This picture shows my family, plus a few other holiday makers in an open-topped coach known as a 'charabanc'. Every day the charabanc would take people off on day trips around the island.

BUTLIN'S HOLIDAY CAMPS

In 1936 Billy Butlin opened the first Butlin's holiday camp in Skegness. It was a totally new way to have a holiday. You paid a single price which covered food, accommodation and entertainment.

• When Billy Butlin's first holiday camp opened, a week there cost £2. Today it would cost between £50 and £100.

Arthur

My family had a boat which we kept on the west coast of Scotland. She was **60** feet (20m) long, but was by no means the largest on the Clyde in those days. We had many happy holidays sailing amongst the islands. Two fishermen acted as crew and my brother and sisters and I enjoyed helping them. Great care had to be taken with the huge sails to prevent them getting mildew. The boat was very well cared for with well-scrubbed decks and shiny polished brassware.

Arthur's early love of sailing led to him joining the Royal Navy when he left school.

TRANSPORT

HORSE-DRAWN VEHICLES

The 1930s was probably the last decade when horse-drawn traffic was still a common sight to see. Small companies often used horse-drawn vehicles to deliver goods locally.

Bob

This picture shows the horse and wagon that my dad used to deliver goods from my grandfather's hardware shop. The horse was used until the early thirties when it was replaced with a van.

Towards the end of the thirties, vans started to take the place of horse-drawn transport.

A Leicester milk van in 1938.

TRAMS

Few people had cars at the beginning of the 1930s. Short journeys like shopping or going to school were made on foot or by bicycle. Longer journeys were made by bus, tram or train.

Every big town had a tram service. Trams were a curious mixture of both trains and buses. They ran on metal rails laid down the middle of most streets, but were directed by policemen, like buses and other traffic.

Arthur

Glasgow was famous for its tram system. The trams got their power from electric wires overhead. When the tram reached its destination, it did not turn around. The driver walked from the front to the back carrying his throttle and brake handles, and the back end now became the front. I travelled to school by tram - the fare was one penny. Children often jumped on and off trams while they were moving. The conductor did not seem to mind, and often helped haul you on board.

BIKES

For many people in the thirties, the bicycle was the only form of transport. Children cycled to school and many people cycled to work. Most postmen and policemen did their jobs by bike.

Joyce

My family did not have a car of their own but my grandparents had a beautiful car. It was an Armstrong Siddeley and it was a great treat to go for a ride in it.

CARS

By the end of the decade, cars were being mass-produced in Britain. Austin, Morris, Triumph and Rover were some of the early makes. Although cars were fairly cheap, a new car was still too expensive for most families.

THEN & NOW

• A new family car cost between £100 and £200 in the thirties. Now a similar sized car would cost over £10,000.

BOATS

Passenger boats were often powered by steam. A steamship was a huge liner that could carry over a thousand people. A trip to America took at least four days.

Arthur

When we went on holiday we went by paddle steamer. The steamer was powered by steam from coal-fired boilers. The engine room was full of a wonderful array of shiny copper pipes, pumps and pistons. It was fun to watch when the steamer was arriving or leaving a pier, because the engineers had to reverse the huge pistons. At this time you could see inside the paddle boxes and it was like looking into a huge washing machine.

THE SECOND WORLD WAR

On Sunday 3 September 1939, people crowded around their wireless sets to hear Prime Minister Neville Chamberlain speak to the country. He said, 'I have to tell you that this country is now at war with Germany.' People had been expecting a war for more than a year and many thought air raids and gas attacks would begin straight away.

Norman

On the 4 September 1939, the day after war was declared, my mother and sister and I left London to stay with my aunt Pauline in Bournemouth. Everyone was very worried that London would be bombed. In fact nothing happened until the next year and so we all returned home after a few weeks. People came to call this the 'phoney war'. This picture shows us walking along the front in Bournemouth.

After the initial worry and panic, the war actually started very quietly and there was no fighting until the summer of 1940. However, the decade came to an uneasy end with many young men leaving home to fight in the Second World War, and with their families not knowing when or if they would return.

FURTHER READING

History From Objects - *At School, In the Street, Keeping Clean* and *Toys*, Hodder Wayland

History From Photographs - *Clothes and Uniforms, Houses and Homes, Journeys, People Who Help Us, School, In the Home* and *In the Street,* Hodder Wayland

Take Ten Years - *1930s,* Evans Brothers 1991

20th Century Fashion -*20s and 30s, Flappers and Vamps*; Cally Blackman, Heinemann, 1999

Travelling in Grandma's Day, Faye Gardner, Evans Brothers 1997

Fiction:
The Family from One End Street, Eve Garnett, Puffin

GLOSSARY

accumulator: A type of rechargeable battery used in early wirelesses.

boarding house: An inexpensive hotel, usually at the seaside.

copper: A large bowl, originally made of copper, with a fire underneath, that was used for doing the laundry.

council: A local governing organization.

decimalization: The introduction of a new system of money in 1971.

ironmonger: A shop selling tools, building materials and household implements.

mangle: A machine with rollers for squeezing water out of wet laundry.

National Health Service: A service set up in 1948 which aimed to give free health care to everybody.

pasteurization: The sterilization of milk by heat.

perishable goods: Foods that are likely to decay quickly.

power station: A place that generates electricity, often from burning coal.

quarantine: A period of isolation to prevent the spread of illness.

shilling: An amount of money worth 12 old pence (5p).

slum housing: Very poor or run-down housing.

suburbs: The area of housing outside a city centre.

tuberculosis: A dangerous and infectious disease.

unemployed: Without a job.

wireless: A radio set.

INDEX